Tibetan

PRAYER FLAGS

Tibetan
PRAYER FLAGS

Send your blessings on the breeze

Text and photographs Diane Barker
Consultant Dru-gu Choegyal Rinpoche

CONNECTIONS
BOOK PUBLISHING

DEDICATION

I dedicate this book with love to the Tibetan people.
May their culture flourish for the benefit of all beings.

A CONNECTIONS EDITION
This edition published in Great Britain in 2003 by
Connections Book Publishing Limited
St Chad's House, 148 King's Cross Road, London WCIX 9DH

This edition published in the U.S.A. in 2003 by
Connections Book Publishing Limited.
Distributed in the U.S.A. by Red Wheel/Weiser,
368 Congress Street, Boston, MA 02210

Photographs copyright © Diane Barker 2003
Prayer flag design copyright © Tsering Wanhgchuk 2003
This edition copyright © Eddison Sadd Editions 2003

British Library Cataloguing-in-Publication data available on request.

ISBN 1-85906-106-0

3 5 7 9 10 8 6 4 2

Phototypeset in Centaur using Quark XPress on Apple Macintosh

Origination by United Graphic Pte Ltd, Singapore
Printed by International Print-O-Pac Ltd. India.

Contents

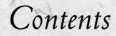

Foreword

As this wonderful book on *lung-ta* flies around the world like a prayer flag, I am grateful and happy to have the opportunity to offer prayers, with love and respect, for all beings in the entire universe.

Prayer flags are a very important aspect of Tibetan culture. They can be seen flying all over the Tibetan plateau, and throughout the year the wind carries their many prayers to all corners of our earth. Prayer flags act as a reminder to Tibet that it should remain an example of a land with a true understanding of the Buddha's teachings – a land of peace, love and prosperity, free from hatred, that can promote harmony and joy beyond its borders.

To hang prayer flags is always a virtuous action, no matter where they are placed. Tibetans always hang flags in holy places. The prayers are rich with colours and energy and fly in all directions. Prayer flags flying high with the wind awaken the mind and help to bring a radiance and clarity of thought. Prayer flags are messengers from the heavens to remind the world to move towards peace, harmony and happiness. They also act as an invitation to the heavens to bring benefit both to the living and the dead. Prayer flags bring energy, health, good luck and success, and each flag is like a star on the earth.

Through the prayer flags, I send love and prayers for the situation in Tibet, for true understanding and compassion between the Tibetans and the Chinese, so that they can generate an attitude of deep respect and caring for each other. I would also like to express my deep gratitude to India for having supported the preservation of Tibetan culture outside Tibet in an atmosphere of freedom. May these prayer flags bring peace, happiness and joy across the world, together with development and progress according to each condition.

DRU-GU CHOEGYAL RINPOCHE
Spiritual Head of Tho Dru-gu region, Kham, Tibet

Introduction
Peace and Compassion

". . . one day, some wood-collectors and herdsmen with pure vision and good karma saw me flying through the sky. I was coming from the direction of Mount Kailash, holding in each of my hands a white prayer-flag. They saw me land on the summit of the Crystal Peak, plant the prayer-flags, and fly away. They told the local people, who went to investigate. Everyone could see, on the top of Crystal Peak, a large white prayer-flag that hadn't been there before. This event aroused great faith and caused auspicious circumstances for the Dharma to flourish in that area."

The Life of Shabkar translated by MATTHIEU RICARD

My FASCINATION WITH TIBETAN culture began in the 1970s, when friends introduced me to the imposing figure of the sixteenth Karmapa, who was visiting Britain at the time. This meeting, which took place in a Welsh farmhouse, completely altered the course of my life and work. Later, my travels in India and Nepal brought me into contact with communities of Tibetan exiles, which increased my love of these people and their culture. I eventually travelled to Tibet itself, staying among the nomad communities of Amdo and Kham in the east. The profoundly spiritual

Prayer flags for sale in the Barkhor market outside the Jokhang Temple, Tibet's holiest shrine, in Lhasa.

6

Introduction

focus that imbues Tibetan society and the people's vibrant way of expressing their beliefs, deeply inspired me, feeding a hunger for the transcendent, and for colour and ritual, that was not satis-fied by my own culture. Wherever I found Tibetan communities, I also found constant reminders of prayer and

In the Taerlung area of Kham, a nomad woman spins her prayer wheel in the half-light of her tent.

Boudhnath in Nepal each evening. And everywhere lines of flags inscribed with prayers, mantras and sacred images gaily fluttered.

Prayer flags have long given me a sense of homecoming — wherever I see them, I know I will find Tibetans. In fact, all over the world, lines of prayer

devotion and a concern for the sacred — from monks and nuns emerging from *pujas* clutching their *pechas*, to old people spinning hand-held prayer wheels, from the young woman selling bread who recited mantras under her breath as she served me, to whole families fingering their *malas* in the annual *mani* prayer ceremony in the main temple in Dharamsala in India. There were the crowds of Tibetans circumambulating the *stupa* at

flags sending their messages of peace and compassion for all beings on the wind are a visible indication that Tibetans have settled in that place or that their culture has had an influence there or is respected. I've seen prayer flags in Tibet on the high passes, strung across rivers and attached to nomad's tents; in northern India, fluttering on temple roof tops; in Nepal, for sale on the street stalls; in Scotland, hanging from a *stupa*; and

8

in London's Peace Garden and, of course, they are tied from tree to tree in my own English garden.

These flags symbolize all that Tibetan culture represents for me — a continual awareness of the transcendent and the sacred that permeates our material world, yet somehow remains beyond it. The gradual fading and tattering of the thin cotton material reminds me of the impermanence of life, and of my own mortality. The continual hanging of new flags next to the old ones speaks of renewal and rebirth.

As a potent symbol, prayer flags offer a poetic and spiritual contribution to the peace and well-being of the world, but what of their origins and deeper meaning? To understand more we must look back to the beginnings of Tibetan culture.

BON AND BUDDHISM

Now home to arguably one of the most deeply religious and peace-loving cultures on earth, Tibet in earlier times was inhabited by a fierce warrior people. They practised Bon shamanism, a folk religion based on the worship of nature. It viewed the landscape as sacred, and its practice involved the harnessing, use or subjugation of the natural elements. The sky, mountains, rivers and lakes were believed to be animated by gods, demons or spirits, all of whom demanded careful ritual propitiation in return for protecting the local community.

Tibet was transformed by the establishment of Buddhism in the seventh century, at which time the country was a great military power, a succession of kings having expanded its boundaries far beyond its present borders. Songtsen Gampo, the most remarkable of these kings, married two Buddhist princesses — one Nepalese and one Chinese — and they are credited with introducing Buddhism to the Tibetan court. Buddhism was seen as a civilizing influence, and in the eighth century, King Trisong Detsen sought to promote it, inviting the Indian abbot Shantarakshita to Tibet to found a monastery. However, unable to overcome the opposition of the Bon shamanists, the King, on the advice of Shantarakshita, asked the great Indian tantric yogi Padmasambhava to assist. There are legends of his taming of the local gods and spirits, and of their subsequent conversion to Buddhism as protective deities, and eventually the first monastery, Samye, was built.

Tibetan Buddhist culture is extraordinarily rich; here monks perform a sacred cham *dance at Chung Lung Gonpa in Kham.*

By the end of the eighth century, Buddhism had largely supplanted the native Bon shamanism, while tolerating and absorbing many of its characteristics. Gradually, Buddhism's values and goals filtered through to every aspect of daily life and shaped the aspirations of the people. With the rise of the great monasteries, religious leaders came to play an increas-ingly important role and eventually, with Mongol intervention, a priestly kingship was established – this was the institution of the Dalai Lamas, whose succession was decided by reincarnation. Tibetan expansionism ceased and, with some ups and downs, the nation gradually retreated into its harsh mountain fastness to focus with intense dedication on advanced Buddhist learning, the exploration and understanding of the inner world and the development of the ideals of peace and compassion.

The result was a culture of tremendous depth and richness: today, Tibetan Buddhism is an extraordinary fusion of deep religious study with the colour and ritual of shamanism; a devotion to the sanctity and

"As I walked across the top of the pass, into Tibet, I saw that among the little prayer flags which Tibetans always like to fly in high places, enormous red flags of China had been hoisted, and portraits of Mao Tse-Tung. No doubt this was meant as a welcome, but it was a melancholy welcome to my own country."

H.H. THE DALAI LAMA: *My Land and My People*

power of natural places and practices such as sky burial, pilgrimage, turning prayer wheels and constructing spirit traps, coexists alongside studious monasticism.

THE 'LAND OF SNOWS' REVEALED

So between the eighth and eighteenth centuries, with some internal struggles, Tibet developed its Buddhist culture largely isolated from the outside world. During this time, the 'Land of the Snows' on the roof of the world was more or less closed to outsiders, and became the stuff of myth and legend. Towards the end of the nineteenth century, however, its strategic position in Asia made it a pawn in the 'Great Game' – the struggle between British India, Russia and China for power in the region. The collapse of the Chinese empire and the rise of communism led to a deterioration in China's previously good relationship with Tibet, then Britain began to withdraw from India, and around the same time Russia was forced to focus on troubles at home. Without a strong army and with a somewhat naive and complacent attitude, Tibet was now extremely vulnerable. Between 1949 and 1950 Chinese communist troops invaded the eastern provinces of Amdo and Kham. By 1959 the whole country was controlled by China, and the Dalai Lama had fled to safety in India, along with thousands of his people.

One paradoxical effect of Tibet's devastation by the Chinese and the subsequent scattering of many of its people has been that, through contact with the Tibetan diaspora, Westerners have benefited from its sophisticated Buddhist-centred culture. Tibet's tragic loss of independence has been our gain, as high lamas, like the sixteenth Karmapa, began to come to the West to share their wisdom with societies that they found to be materially rich, but inwardly impoverished.

FLYING HIGH, RUNNING FAST

Scholars have many differing theories about the origin of prayer flags, or *lung-ta*. From my investigations it would seem that they predate Buddhism in Tibet, evolving through an integration of Buddhist practices from India with the pre-Buddhist Bon shamanism.

Bon shamanism has long believed in the concept of *lung-ta*, which represents a person's vital energy and fortune, which is symbolized by a horse or the wind. When their *lung-ta* is large, a person can achieve renown and be successful in their undertakings. To create positive energy which would increase their *lung-ta*, people used eagle or white vulture feathers, symbolizing the power of unstoppable energy flying high, and they drew horses on to cloth to symbolize speed. They would position these decorated cloths and featheres in high places, such as roof tops or mountain passes, where the wind would carry the aspirations of these totems into the heavens. It is thought that, from the earliest times, the Bon *lung-ta* bore the message "May the horse of good fortune run fast and increase the power of life, influence, fortune, wealth and health." They were also inscribed with *"Lha-gyel-lo"* (victory to the gods), which I have heard Tibetans shouting as they go over mountain passes. In pre-Buddhist times, flags were also used as a symbol of power. The Tibetan national flag and those representing the king were red, while the army and the various powerful tribes all had their own coloured flags, each distinguished with an animal or bird symbol.

THE FIRST FLAGS

Meanwhile, according to Indian legend, during his lifetime the Buddha Shakyamuni ascended to the 33rd heaven to teach the dharma to his mother, who had been reborn there. While there, he was asked by Indra, king of that heaven, for help to win over the jealous and aggressive Asuras, who were going to war against the peaceful gods, or Devas. The Buddha gave a teaching on the nature of peace. Known as the Victory Banner Sutra, it was designed to overcome hatred and to bring about understanding and harmony on both the inner and outer planes. He instructed Indra to repeat this sutra in order to achieve victory over all obstacles and enemies. Indra did this with great success.

The Buddha's heavenly disciples eventually brought this sutra to the human realm, where it became popular with Buddhists in India, Afghanistan, China, Dunhuang and Tibet. It is thought that the sutra was first used on banners in India, and this is most likely to be the origin of Buddhist prayer flags.

"I also accepted one hundred lengths of cloth of various colours, with which I made a thousand prayer flags printed with the mani. When I hung them they were enough to make five lines of flags between two hills above my place."

The Life of Shabkar translated by MATTHIEU RICARD

THE POWER OF MANTRA

In the course of establishing his empire, the seventh-century Tibetan king, Songtsen Gampo, came into contact with the Buddhist traditions of India, Khotan and China, and under the influence of his two Buddhist queens, he immersed himself in spiritual pursuits. Avalokiteshvara, the Bodhisattva of compassion, whose sutra came from India, particularly inspired him. This sutra instructs that to print, carve or paint the mantra *"Om mani padme hum"* (Hail to the jewel in the lotus) on to surfaces will benefit many beings through their seeing it and through the action of the elements. This mantra is considered to be the essence of the Buddha's compassion for all beings, and the sutra explains that each of its syllables has a specific and potent effect in bringing about purification and transformation at different levels of our being.

Songtsen Gampo promoted Avalokiteshvara's teachings throughout Tibet: he encouraged people to carve the mantra on to stones and rocks in the countryside and on to wood for use in buildings; he also encouraged them to make prints of it and to hang these as prayer flags. To this day, this is the most popular mantra in the Tibetan cultural world and it can be seen and heard everywhere – Tibetans continually repeat *"Om mani padme hum"* while turning prayer wheels with these words embossed on the outside; it is painted on to rock faces or incised into them, and the syllables are carved on to yak skulls and stones, which are then piled up to form cairns and walls. His holiness the Dalai Lama is considered to be the living incarnation of Avalokiteshvara.

GOOD FORTUNE AND COMPASSION

During his reign Songtsen Gampo designed and promoted a new prayer flag that combined elements from Bon traditions and those of the newly arrived Buddhism. The flag featured the symbols of the windhorse and the four mythical animals – the dragon, snow lion, tiger and garuda – which came from the Bon side, and may have evolved from the symbols used by the different Tibetan clans or from local legend. (The dragon, for example, was present in folklore from earliest times, but it was also well-known in Chinese astrology and art, of which the royal court would have been aware.) The phrase *"Lha-gyel-lo"* was used in the design. Although it has Bon origins, Buddhism has many similar sayings. The sacred mantra of Avalokiteshvara was also added, as was the Victory Banner Sutra.

In this way Songtsen Gampo married together two concepts. On one level, the prayer flags were considered to help an individual's *lung-ta*, or fortune. On another, higher level, the flags would benefit the spiritual life (and future lives) of the person hanging them, and the lives of all living beings wherever the wind carried the powerful mantras and sutras. The flags thus addressed both personal concerns and the need for universal compassion.

A MANTRA FOR OUR TIME

At around the same time, the Buddha Akshobya Sutra, taught during the lifetime of the Buddha Shakyamuni, also came to Tibet from India. This sutra contains a powerful mantra (shown on page 16), said to have been created by all the Buddhas from their compassion, wisdom and power, and originally manifesting in the form of sound and light. It was believed that the mantra would purify and transform the anger of anyone who recited, remembered or saw it. It was also believed that any living being who saw this mantra before dying would be reborn in heaven due to its power, even if they died in a state of rage.

The Buddha Akshobya Mantra was also painted or inscribed wherever people could see it, and was eventually printed on to cloth, becoming another important element of prayer flags.

Emphasising the transformation of anger, this powerful mantra seems extraordinarily relevant in our own disturbed times. In Tibet it is frequently seen painted on banners that are hung for the benefit of animals in places where they are slaughtered.

STYLES, SIZES AND COLOURS

Over time prayer flags evolved into many styles and sizes. Today, the most common is a horizontal line of symbols, mantras and so on printed on to five different coloured pieces of cloth – blue, white, red, green and yellow. These colours represent the five elements – sky, clouds, fire, water (or wood) and earth. They also symbolize the five Buddha families, five directions, five wisdoms and the five mental attributes. In remote areas of Tibet, it is common to see lines of simple white

ནམོརཏྣཏྲཡཡ།ཨོཾཀཾཀནིཀཾཀནི།རོཙནིརོཙནི།ཏྲོཏནིཏྲོཏནི།ཏྲསནིཏྲསནི།
པྲཏིཧནཔྲཏིཧན།སརྦཀརྨཔརཾཔ་རནྫེམེསརྦསཏྟོནནྱཙྪསྭཧཱ།

Namo ratna trayaya	*To the Three Jewels I prostrate*
Om kamkani kamkani	*No sin, no sin,*
Rotsani rotsani	*No burning, no burning,*
Trotsani trotsani	*No shattering, no shattering,*
Trasani trasani	*No fear, no fear,*
Pratihana pratihana	*No scattering, no scattering,*
Sarva karma parampara	*All the chains of the constant flow of karma,*
Nime sarva sato	*since beginningless time, are broken,*
Nanyatsa soaha	*May it be accomplished.*

Believed to have been created by all the Buddhas from their compassion,
wisdom and power, the Buddha Akshobya Mantra is highly revered and very powerful.

flags, as the local people cannot afford to print on to coloured cloth.

As well as the horizontal lines of *lung-ta*, there are also long vertical flags, attached to bamboo poles and known as *darchen*, which can be made of coloured or white cloth. In many places in Tibet it is possible to see very long horizontal yellow flags called *serzam* (or golden bridges) which are hung across roads or over streams and rivers, to benefit all the beings (including the *naga*, or water spirits) who would pass underneath. In the spirit of compassion, a Tibetan friend of mine hoped to hang a 'golden bridge' across the river Danube in Vienna but he discovered that local bylaws would not allow him to execute this plan.

In eastern Tibet I have seen many *darpung*. These are white prayer flags beautifully arranged to form a pyramid shape. *Darpung* are sometimes erected where people have died in an accident, but they can also mark the spot where a lama has given teachings or where an important person was cremated.

PRAYERS, MANTRAS AND INVOCATIONS

There are many other typical prayer flags, rich with images of Buddhist deities and traditional Tibetan symbols. They bear a multitude of prayers, mantras and invocations for a variety of purposes — such as the promotion of good health, for longevity or for protection while travelling — as well as being for the greater spiritual benefit of all living beings.

Particularly popular are flags bearing the image of White or Green Tara, the most beloved of the female deities in Tibetan Buddhism, and prayers and mantras related to them. It is said that in his sorrow at the pain of samsara, two tears fell from the eyes of Avalokiteshvara and that these were transformed into the two Taras due to the blessings of all the Buddhas. White Tara represents the motherly aspect of compassion, and Green Tara, who is always shown with one leg extended as if about to step down, represents the active form of compassion — she is believed to come to the aid of supplicants very quickly. Buddhism is not theistic — the deities represent enlightened aspects of ourselves, archetypes to which we aspire to connect.

Also common are flags showing the image of Tibet's great sage, the tantric yogi Padmasambhava, accompanied by associated prayers and mantras, and recently there has been an enthusiasm for flags featuring the Kalachakra monogram, which symbolizes the highest of all tantric initiations conducted for world peace. Popular among certain communities in eastern Tibet are *lung-ta* bearing the image of Ling Gesar, a popular epic hero and the subject of a host of magical songs and stories in the country's folk tradition.

From time to time new flags appear, sometimes prompted by the dream-visions of high lamas. For example, the sixteenth Karmapa had a dream in which *dakinis* showed him a flag which he was encouraged to create. The resulting very bold and simple flag is known as the 'Karmapa Dream Flag' and features two abstracted wave shapes in yellow and turquoise, symbolizing peace and harmony. The present Karmapa

has also created a new flag as a protection against earthquakes — something to which the Himalayan region is very prone!

PRINTING AND HANGING

Traditionally, skilled wood-block carvers, usually monks or lamas, produced prayer flag blocks as a spiritual practice. These days the blocks are just as likely to be carved by lay people, such as the expert craftsmen and their apprentices of the small exile Khampa community of Tashi Jong in northern India, who produce beautiful and intricate designs for printing prayer flags. The blocks would then be inked and the images transferred on to cloth flags, which are then sewn on to rope for hanging.

Many Tibetan families have their own blocks that have been handed down for generations, and they use these for making sets of flags. When I mentioned prayer-flag printing to my elderly lama friend, Jamyang-la, he vanished into his room to rummage in

"…I purify the Lord of the Lungta of the North
with his retinue of nine hundred and ten thousand (deities of fortune)
with the smoke of the five (aromatic) plants.
I offer him clean shobu made of the substance of cereals
And for him I set up a white flag as support:
Develop the lungta and spread fame!
Make this adverse fortune propitious!
I raise the great banner of merit and glory!
I set up the crest banner with the vulture feathers of fame!
May this fortune resound like thunder in the three spheres of existence! "

NAMKHAI NORBU RINPOCHE: *Drung, Deu and Bon*

a trunk and emerged with his own old block — burnished and blackened through decades of inking — respectfully wrapped in layers of cloth and newspaper.

Before hanging new sets of prayer flags, Tibetans will often take them to be blessed by a lama, who recites prayers and mantras over them for added auspiciousness, and quite often the hoisting of flags will also be accompanied by a smoke purification ritual. Called *zamling ji sang* and originating in Bon times, this involves making prayers to various deities, while burning fragrant substances — most commonly juniper boughs mixed with other scented woods and incense —

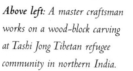

Above left: A master craftsman works on a wood-block carving at Tashi Jong Tibetan refugee community in northern India.

Above: Sewing newly printed flags on to rope in Dharamsala, India.

Left: In a Dharamasala workshop prayer flags are printed using an inked wood block. Behind are new sets of flags, ready for hanging.

which bless the flags and purify the surrounding area. In Kham my Tibetan friends and I hung new flags while a local lama conducted this ritual as an offering to the local mountain deity.

The placing of prayer flags traditionally depends on many factors, and can be influenced by the needs of the person who hangs them, by astrology, by geomancy and by the requirements of the wider community at a particular time. As mentioned before, they are most frequently hung in elevated places such as on mountain tops and high passes and the roof tops and eaves of homes and temples. They can also be hung across rivers, at pilgrimage places, from bridges and from nomad tents.

The flags that can be seen in cemeteries and places of sky burial or cremation are known as *jodar* rather than *lung-ta* — *lung-ta* referring to a person's life force and, therefore, inappropriate for someone who is deceased. *Jodar* generally bear only Buddhist mantras and are white.

"*... since I was born in the Wood Hog Year, and wood is green, astrologers would have said that green was my lucky colour. Indeed, for that reason my personal prayer flags were green, and they were flying from the roof of my house and beginning to stir in a gentle morning breeze.*"

H.H. THE DALAI LAMA: *My Land and My People*

AUSPICIOUS TIMES

The early hours of the morning, when the energy of the day is symbolically pure and fresh, are considered to be the most auspicious time for any new endeavour and thus also for the hanging of prayer flags, and they are often hoisted at other times of significant new

continued on page 24

Nechung Kuden-la, the medium of the state oracle of Tibet, blesses prayer flags at Nechung monastery, Dharamsala.

YOUR TIBETAN PRAYER FLAG DESIGN

The 'Windhorse', probably the best-known type of prayer flag, has been specially re-designed by the master artist Tsering Wanhgchuk to accompany this book. He has used the following symbols and mantras that represent the blessings you will be sending on the breeze.

WINDHORSE *The horse represents the earth element, yellow, and the wisdom of equanimity. On its back is a wish-fulfilling jewel, symbolizing the three jewels of the dharma — the Buddha, Dharma and the Sangha. In the corners are mythical animals, known as the four dignities or the guardians of the four directions:* GARUDA, *or Kyung, a mythical bird, represents the wind element, green, and all accomplishing wisdom;* DRAGON, *or Druk, represents the space element, blue, and all-encompasssing wisdom;* SNOW LION, *or Senge, represents the water element, white, and mirror-like wisdom;* TIGER, *or Tag, represents the fire element, red, and discriminating wisdom.*

TOP PANEL *The eight symbols of good fortune: Parasol, Golden Fishes, Treasure Vase, Lotus, Conch Shell, Endless Knot, Victory Banner, Wheel.*

BOTTOM PANEL *The seven jewels of royal power: Precious Wheel, Jewel, Queen, Minister, Elephant, Horse, General.*

LEFT AND RIGHT SCROLLS *The scrolls contain the eight sources of good fortune.* Left: *Mirror, Conch Shell, Durva Grass, Yoghurt.* Right: *Cinnabar, Bezoar Medicine, Bilva Fruit, Mustard Seeds.*

TOP MANTRA
Om muni muni maha munaye sva ha
Mantra of all the Buddhas to generate love, energy and wisdom for all beings.
Om vajra guru padma siddhi hum
Mantra of Padmasambhava to eliminate the negative forces of the dark age.

LEFT MANTRA
Om a midheva hri
Mantra of Amitabha, the Buddha of infinite life and light.
Om a ra pa ca na dhi
Mantra of Manjusri, the embodiment of wisdom.
Om vajrasattva hum
Short mantra of Vajrasattva, the embodiment of purity and awakening.
Om ta re tutta re ture sva ha
Mantra of Tara, the female embodiment of protection.

RIGHT MANTRA
Om mani padme hum
Mantra of Avalokiteshvara, the embodiment of love and compassion.
Hum vajra phet
Mantra of Vajrapani, the wrathful being who eliminates harmful influences.
Om vajrasattva hum
Continuation of the mantra of Vajrasattva.
Om ta re ta sva ha
Short mantra of Tara (see above).

BOTTOM MANTRA
Ah ka sa ma ra tsa sha da rah sa mah ra ya phet
The heart syllable of the supreme female energy of enlightenment — may your lifespan, merit, glory, wealth, physical energy, power and health rise up like the windhorse.
Lha-gyel-lo! *Victory to the gods! A prayer to enlist support for the health, happiness and peace of the entire world.*

TOP PANEL

GARUDA

TOP MANTRA

LEFT MANTRA

LEFT SCROLL

WINDHORSE

SNOW LION

BOTTOM PANEL

DRAGON

RIGHT MANTRA

RIGHT SCROLL

BOTTOM MANTRA

TIGER

23

beginnings, such as birth, at marriage ceremonies and at the start of long journeys. One of the favourite periods for the hanging of new *lung-ta* is in the first few days after the celebratory time of *Losar*, Tibetan New Year, which falls in February or March. The fifteenth day of the fifth Tibetan month, known as World Peace Day and coinciding with summer picnic season, is the most popular time for hoisting flags in Kham, in eastern Tibet.

Many Tibetans consult astrologers to find favourable days for putting up *lung-ta* – not only for increasing their personal good fortune, but also to deal with obstacles, quarrels and disease.

The type of flag chosen will be determined by the situation and the colour used is often decided by the element that rules the year of the person's birth. Many flags have blank spaces on so that they can be personalized by adding a name and birth year. I learned from Tibetan astrologers that particular flags can even be used around the borders of a village to ward off an epidemic or to protect against floods in the monsoon season. In the same way, prayer flags can be used for geomantic purposes, to balance the energies in areas with unfavourable environmental circumstances.

According to an old Tibetan text there are also inauspicious days for raising prayer flags. These are called Bhaden days, when negative forces prevail and obstacles can be created. They are linked with the waxing and waning of the moon and are calculated on an annual basis by Tibetan astrologers.

WHEN TO HANG YOUR FLAGS

Here in the West we can raise prayer flags to mark, celebrate and bless weddings, births, new ventures and any meaningful days in our personal lives, as well as important days in our own spiritual tradition. We can hang them to protect against dangers and negative influences, for example when a friend or relative is ill, or to overcome obstacles and increase prosperity and encourage a long life. Most importantly, because of

Early in the morning a Tibetan attaches new prayer flags to a tree behind the Dalai Lama's residence in Dharamsala.

their powerful invocations of wisdom and compassion, we can hang them to send our prayers for peace and harmony on the wind to all beings everywhere. Rigpa, an organization set up to promote Tibetan Buddhism in the West, publishes an annual and inexpensive 'Tibetan Calendar', which is a useful guide for anyone concerned about Bhaden, or inauspicious, days. It is obtainable from any of their centres, see page 64.

Tibetans recommend that new flags are hung in the early morning, and that we carry clear, positive and altruistic intentions as we hang them. As the symbols and mantras on the prayer flags are sacred, they request that we should treat them with respect and not place them on the ground, stand on them or use them in any inappropriate way. If we need to dispose of old flags, we should burn them, releasing their last expression of prayer to the atmosphere.

Prayer flags can be hung inside or out, wherever a breeze will catch them and transmit their blessings. We can make our own small contribution to world peace by hanging them from house eaves or balconies, across gateways, along paths, above doorways and from tree to tree, and particularly in special areas designed for peace and contemplation. As it represents the sky, the blue flag is usually arranged to hang slightly higher than the others.

You can also make your own prayer flags. All you need is some fine cotton cloth and markers or fabric paints. You can reproduce your favourite prayers or inspirational poems or create your own new blessings for the world. Decorate the cloth with patterns and designs or personal symbols – using paint, appliqué, printing stamps or glitter. Choegyal Rinpoche, my consultant on this book, suggests designing a prayer flag for our times. It can contain mantras, prayers and symbols from many great faiths, thus bringing them together in a spirit of peace and harmony. Don't forget to leave a margin at the top of the flags for sewing them on to twine! Above all, create prayer flags with the right motivation and you too will benefit from their blessings.

Blessings on the Breeze

My fascination with Tibetan culture has grown alongside my love for the
people during my visits to Tibetan communities both inside and outside Tibet.
At these times I have always been surrounded by prayer flags.
My photographs on the following pages show the flags in use throughout
the Tibetan cultural world.

*P*rayer flags on the lingkhor
around the Dalai Lama's residence
in Dharamsala, northern India.
Dharamsala, formerly a British
hill station, has been the home
of the Dalai Lama and base of
the Tibetan Government in exile
since 1960. During this time,
it has attracted thousands
of refugees, as well as
pilgrims, from Tibet.

Lung-ta suspended across the Dri Chu (Yangtze) river south of Derge in Kham, eastern Tibet. Hanging flags above water will benefit all the beings that pass underneath. I learned that there are no bridges for some considerable distance in this area. To visit family members on the other side, locals have to risk their lives by crossing the turbulent waters in coracles.

Prayer flags erected at Tabo Gonpa in Spiti, in northern India. The occasion was the Kalachakra Initiation Ceremony led by the Dalai Lama in 1996 as part of the 1000th anniversary celebrations of the founding of the temple. The Kalachakra initiation is believed to bring peace and harmony and reduce all tension and violence in the world.

31

A wealth of prayer
flags hanging behind
Thekchen Choling, the
Dalai Lama's residence in
Dharamsala. Green is the
auspicious colour of the
Dalai Lama as determined
by astrology, and along
with most of the other
flags, it is likely that the
green flags would have been
raised on a Wednesday —
considered his astrologically
lucky day.

A carver of mani stones attracts a crowd on the lingkhor around Kalden Jampaling monastery in Chamdo, Kham. Mani stones are not only incised with the sacred mantra of Avalokiteshvara, but can also be decorated with skilfully rendered images of deities, as here. Chamdo was the tragic scene of the Tibetan army's capitulation to the communist Chinese in 1950.

Prayer flags crackling in the wind above nomad grasslands near Hongyuan in Amdo, Tibet. New prayer flags also flutter from the tops of the tents below, erected to honour the recent teachings given in the area by a travelling lama. From their nearby tents my nomad friends and I visited this latse, on the way collecting wild raspberries in the remnant of forest below.

*Fragrant juniper smoke veils
lung-ta lines in Dharamsala.
Called zampling ji sang,
the juniper burning ritual,
originates from Bon texts.
These state that purifying
goddesses manifested in the
form of sacred plants, such
as juniper. When these plants
were burnt, the energy and
blessings of the goddesses
would emerge as smoke,
purifying and energizing
the surrounding area.*

*A*n elderly lama hangs new flags on the roof of Khaspang Retreat Centre in honour of the imminent arrival of an important Rinpoche. Khaspang is situated at the end of the remote Igu Valley, on the edge of the Changthang Desert in Ladakh. Solitary retreat is an important aspect of Tibetan Buddhist practice and committed practitioners can spend many years, or even a lifetime, in retreat.

A cairn of mani stones and prayer flags on the Namshang-la Pass in Ladakh. Invariably, when Tibetans cross a major pass they will stop to tie a new set of prayer flags and burn incense as an offering to the mountain god there. My Tibetan friends would throw paper prayer flags from our jeep window as we rolled over some passes, crying "Lha-gyel-lo!" (see page 22)

*Prayer flags arranged
to form a pyramid, or
darpung, at Taerlung in
Kham. These flags honour
the spot where a high
lama recently gave open-air
teachings. My lama friend
had just been assisting
in the sacred cham dances
at the nearby monastery,
hence his sumptuous jacket.*

*This smoke purification
ritual is an offering to the
local mountain deity and
to bless new flags erected at
Ngawang nga pa in Kham.
An elderly nomad told us
that this mountain deity
had appeared to him when
he was hunting in the
forest as a youth. Terrified,
he threw down his gun and
fled — never to hunt again.*

43

New flags are added to the old on the lingkhor in Dharamsala. Fading and disintegrating with time, prayer flags are a constant reminder of impermanence, and their renewal celebrates new life, reminding us that we are part of nature and the cycle of time.

A new arrival from Tibet
hangs lung-ta behind the
Dalai Lama's home.
He was with a group of
young people hoisting new
flags and I was touched to
see the respect they all had
for the lung-ta. They were
careful not to step on old
flags that had blown down
and took the trouble to lift
them off the ground and
rehang them.

A nun relaxing under her umbrella at Tso Pema, Himachal Pradesh in India. Padmasambhava, the great tantric yogi who helped to establish Buddhism in Tibet, meditated in the caves here with his consort Mandarava. Now, dedicated monks, nuns and lay practitioners live and practise in them.

Lines of flags hang from the trees in Dharamsala. In the background are the Dhauladar Mountains, foothills of the Himalayas. I have heard that, in the early days of his exile from Tibet, the Dalai Lama enjoyed the freedom of trekking into these mountains. This was in sharp contrast to his formative years in Tibet, where due to his role he was mostly confined to the Potala palace in Lhasa.

Among lung-ta in Dharamsala hangs a new flag, conceived and designed by the present Karmapa as a protection against earthquakes, and featuring the Indian tantric yogi Padmasambhava in the centre. The entire Himalayan region is subject to intense geological activity, and earthquakes are a very real threat. Dharamsala is situated in a zone with the highest possible likelihood of seismic activity.

A young Tibetan boy and
his dog play in the Jokhang
Square in Lhasa. The Jokhang
Temple, built in the reign of
Songtsen Gampo on a spot
deemed to be the principal site
of geomantic power in Tibet,
is Tibet's most sacred shrine.
It is a focal point for
pilgrims from all over Tibet,
some of whom spend years
making prostrations en route.

*C*hildren playing
among the prayer flags at
Pema Shelpuk in Kham.
Associated with the
yogi Padmasambhava,
this power place is
an important pilgrimage
site. It is also a terma site,
meaning that an important
sacred text, concealed by
Padmasambhava, was
revealed here centuries
later by a terton, or
treasure finder.

*T*hese children, including
two young monks, are
playing at Karchin healing
spring in Amchok, Amdo.
The spring is considered
to be the gift of the local
female protector deity,
Nidakma, who lives on the
mountaintop above it.
In the bushes are tied not
only prayer flags but
also katag, white silk
offering scarves.

A young man descends
carefully after erecting
new prayer flags behind
Thekchen Choling in
Dharamsala. Monks and
scholars advise that the blue
flag, which always starts
the set of five colours,
should be hung at the
highest point as it
symbolizes the sky.
The other colours are:
white for cloud, red for
fire, green for water and
yellow for earth.

A tangle of flags hanging
from the trees by Tso Pema
(Rewalsar) Lake in
northern India. Both
Tibetan Buddhists and
Hindus revere this small
lake as a sacred site.
On this occasion, devotees
of the young seventeenth
Karmapa, who was on
his first pilgrimage here,
had put up new flags.

57

Stupas festooned with prayer flags in Dechen area, Kham. Stupas (chortens, in Tibetan) signify an object of offering and usually contain the relics of the Buddha or some great spiritual master. Among the peaks in the background is Mount Kawa Karpo, a major power place and another important focus of pilgrimage in eastern Tibet.

A *thread cross at the base of a latse in the south Amdo grasslands of Tibet. Thread crosses have their origins in Bon tradition and during a ritual are used to represent the abode of a deity. They can also be used as a device for trapping and exorcising evil forces.*

"May all who suffer be free from suffering
May all those in fear find freedom from fear
May all who grieve find freedom from grief
May all living beings be free."
THE BUDDHA

Glossary

GLOSSARY

Bhaden days Inauspicious days, when hanging prayer flags is not advisable.

Bhodhisattva One who has the altruistic mind of enlightenment and is on the path to full Buddhahood, but who chooses to remain in the world to eliminate the sufferings of others.

Bon An ancient shamanic spiritual tradition, widespread in Tibet prior to the official introduction and establishment of Buddhism. Bon still exists in Tibet alongside Buddhism, having absorbed many of its characteristics.

Cham Religious dance.

Chorten See **Stupa**.

Dakinis 'Sky dancer', a female embodiment of wisdom.

Darchen Long flags attached to a bamboo pole and flown vertically.

Darpung Flags hung in the shape of a pyramid.

Dharma The truth of the Buddha's teachings; the Buddhist path.

Jodar White flags generally raised in cemeteries or places of sky burial or cremation.

Kalachakra The highest tantric initiation, believed to bring peace and harmony and reduce all tension and violence in the world.

Karmapa The title of the 17 successive incarnations who have headed the Karma Kagyu lineage of Tibetan Buddhism.

Katag Offering scarves made of white silk.

Lama A spiritual teacher or guru.

Latse A cairn of prayer flags on top of a mountain pass.

Lingkhor A holy route of circumambulation around a holy place or person.

Losar Tibetan new year, a holiday time of public ceremonies, cham dances and picnics.

Lung-ta Sets of prayer flags flown in a horizontal line.

Mala A string of 108 prayer beads.

Mani Refers to the mantra *Om mani padme hum.*

Mani stones: Stones inscribed with the mantra of Avalalokiteshvara: *Om mani padme hum.*

Mantra Sacred syllables which can be repeated many times as part of a spiritual practice and which have a powerfully transformative function.

Naga A powerful water spirit.

Pechas Religious texts in loose-leaf form.

Prostration A physical expression of homage to a higher power and a spiritually purifying activity. It involves lying full length on the ground, moving forward one body length and then repeating the procedure, while visualizing the Buddha or a Buddha-deity in front of you.

Puja An offering (or prayer) ceremony.

Rinpoche Meaning 'precious one', a term of respect used by Tibetans for a reincarnate lama.

Samsara The endless cycle of birth, death and rebirth, characterized by suffering due to ignorance.

Serzam Long yellow flags flown horizontally over roads or water. Known as 'golden bridges'.

Sky burial The practice of dismembering human corpses and compassionately feeding the remains to vultures.

Stupa (In Tibetan *chorten*) A shrine that usually contains the relics of the Buddha or some great spiritual master.

Sutra The teachings of the Buddha.

Terma Sacred texts or treasures hidden by Padmasambhava in places of geomantic power on the Tibetan landscape, which are later revealed by a terton.

Terton One whose destiny it is to reveal a sacred text or treasure hidden by Padmasambhava.

Zamling ji sang A prayer and purification ritual involving the burning of fragrant woods.

PEOPLE

Avalokiteshvara: (In Tibetan *Chenresig*) 'Patron deity' of Tibet, the celestial Bodhisattva of compassion.

Buddha Akshobya The Buddha of one of the Five Enlightened Families which correspond to a perfected state of an individual's five faculties. Akshobya represents the transmutation of delusion (or hate) into the mirror-like clarity of wisdom.

Buddha Shakyamuni The historic Buddha, Shakyamuni was born as the Indian prince Siddhartha (sixth to fifth centuries BC) and became the fully enlightened Buddha while meditating under the Bodhi tree in Bodhgaya.

Khampa People from Kham.

Ling Gesar The legendary warrior king, hero of Tibetan epic poetry.

Padmasambhava (In Tibetan *Guru Rinpoche* – Precious Guru.) The great Indian tantric yogi who helped found Buddhism in Tibet.

Samye The first Buddhist monastery in Tibet.

Shantarakshita The Indian abbot invited by King Trisong Detsen to found the first monastery in Tibet.

Songtsen Gampo The great seventh-century Tibetan king who unified the country for the first time and encouraged the introduction of Buddhism into Tibet.

Tara Meaning 'saviouress', Tara is said by one legend to have been born from Avalokiteshvara's tears of compassion for suffering humanity, and in another from her own vow to be enlightened in a woman's body. There are many aspects of Tara – the two most popular are White Tara, who represents the motherly aspect of compassion, and Green Tara, who represents active compassion.

Trisong Detsen The great Tibetan King during whose reign Buddhism was formally established as the state religion.

PLACES

Amdo The north-eastern province of Tibet, an area of high altitude rolling grasslands largely populated by nomads.

Boudnath Name of a great stupa at Boudha, near Kathmandu, Nepal, said to contain the relics of a previous Buddha and now focus of a large Tibetan exile community.

Dharamsala A centre of Tibetan refugees in India, home of the Dalai Lama and base of the Tibetan Government in exile.

Kham One of the three main traditional provinces of Tibet. Covering the south-eastern part of the country, it includes the watersheds of the Salween, Mekong, Yangtse, Yarlung and Gyarong rivers.

BIBLIOGRAPHY

My Land and My People, H.H. the Dalai Lama, Warner Books, USA, 1997.

The Life of Shabkar, translated by Matthieu Ricard, Snow Lion Publications, USA, 2001.

Drung, Deu and Bon, Prof. Namkhai Norbu, Library of Tibetan Works and Archives, India.

The Windhorse and the Well Being of Man, Samten Karme, from *Anthropology in the Himalayas and Tibet*, Volkerkunemuseum der Universitat Zurich, Switzerland, 1990.

The Encyclopedia of Tibetan Symbols and Motifs Robert Beer, Serindia, UK, 1999.

Tibet Handbook, Gyurme Dorje, Footprint Handbooks, UK.

The Sacred Life of Tibet, Keith Dowman, Thorsons, UK, 1997.

The Tibetan Book of Living and Dying, Sogyal Rinpoche, Rider Books, UK, 1992.

Prayer Flags, Acharya Tashi Tsering, *Me-long*, No.7 Dec.

Resources

1990, Newsletter of the Council for Religious and Cultural Affairs of H.H. the Dalai Lama, India, 1990.

RESOURCES

THE TIBET SOCIETY AND TIBET RELIEF FUND UK.
Unit 9, 139 Fonthill Rd,
London N4 3HF
020 7272 1414

TIBET FOUNDATION,
1 St. James Market,
London SW1Y 4SB
020 7930 6001

TIBET HOUSE,
1 Culworth St,
London NW8 7AF
020 7722 5378

WEB SITES:
www.hitherandyononline.com
www.prayerflags.com
www.rigpa.org
www.spirit-of-tibet.co.uk
www.tibet.org
www.tibetsearch.com
www.westwindprayerflags.com
www.choegyalrinpoche.org

ACKNOWLEDGEMENTS

I offer deep gratitude to all the people listed who helped me with this book. All positive aspects of this project come from them – any mistakes and inaccuracies are mine.

Most particularly I would like to thank Dru-gu Choegyal Rinpoche for the blessing of his friendship and support. He generously gave of his time, wisdom, energy and enthusiasm to patiently lead me through the intricacies of the history and meaning of prayer flags and helped me to make sense of all the information I had collected. Thanks also to him for organizing the design of our prayer flag. I have been impressed by Rinpoche's compassion and equanimity towards the Chinese people and by his hopes that Tibetans and Chinese can work together in harmony, with mutual caring and respect, to protect and cherish Tibetan culture for the benefit of everyone. He truly lives the spirit of prayer flags; Tsering Wangchuk, master artist from Tashi Jong Tibetan community in northern India, who designed the authentic and beautiful prayer flag that accompanies this book; Nechung Kuden-la who graciously allowed me to photograph him blessing prayer flags; Jamyang-la for printing a set of prayer flags for me, and his apprentice Dadak for sewing them; the friendly old man on the Holy Walk around the Dalai Lama's palace, whose name I neglected to ask, who allowed me to photograph him printing prayer flags; Pema Yeshe and Tsering Norzom of the Library of Tibetan Works and Archives; Jeremy Russell of the Norbulinka Institute; Karma Rongpo, secretary at Nechung monastery, for his friendship; Mr. Lobsang Norbu Gyalnang and Phurbu Tsering of the Tibetan Astro. Institute, Dharamsala; Ngawangthondup Narkyid, of the Private Office of His Holiness the Dalai Lama; Amchok Choetar for his friendship; Jackie Crovetto, Zara Fleming and Gillian Stokes for reading the first draft; Liz Puttick, my agent, for being such a star; Nick, Ian and Elaine of Eddison Sadd for dreaming up the idea, believing in my part in it, and for being such fun to work with.

The extracts from *The Life of Shabkar* are reproduced by permission of Snow Lion Publications, Ithaca, NY, USA. www.SnowLion.Pub.com

The prayer flags are supplied by Tiger Tiger Inc., PO Box 7341, Berkeley, CA 94707, USA. www.tigertiger.com